SECURE YOUR
INTERNET USE

SECURE YOUR INTERNET USE

Jerome Svigals

To order additional copies of this book, contact:
Xlibris
1-888-795-4274
www.Xlibris.com
Orders@Xlibris.com
733197

CONTENTS

Dedication

Purpose: Identify individuals Assisting Us.
Action: Show appreciation.

A Dedication

As a 22 year old engineer in an 88 year old body, let me first thank the group of professionals that keep me alive and well. They include Drs Gary Aron, Bruce Benedick, Pardis Kelly, Philip Ng and (Mrs) Blanca Vargas of the Powerhouse Gym in Redwood City, CA. Also, many thanks to patent attorney Ed Radlo of Radloip, Los Gatos, CA.

Preface

Purpose: Provide an Introduction to this Book.
Action: Provide background necessary to use this book.

Purpose of this book: The transaction world is quickly evolving from an era of electronic transactions, based on plastic cards and readable checks, to a new era of smart device transactions, based on hand-held, communication's based, stored program operated, transaction devices (Smart Devices) communicating via networks, primarily the world wide Internet.

This book is intended to help you understand the use of Smart Devices on the Internet in preparing for the Internet security challenges. It is intended to introduce you to the Internet and its role, in the Smart Devices era.

Smart Devices Concepts

The hand held communicating smart (programmed) device has introduced a new way of life. It offers walking and traveling conversation. Stand on any street corner, in any city at any time of the day and you will observe all classes of society going bye with a hand held communications device being held next to their ear. Usage statistics claim more than 80% of the world's population have access to and use a communicating phone like device. Their use ranges from socializing and safety to commercial and financial activities. The users range from 8 or 10 years old to immobile senior citizens seeking social interaction and a substitute for physical motion.

Smartphone Based Financial Transactions:

The Smartphone is a hand-held, internet based, stored program computer which includes cell phone functions.

The Internet is a world wide network of computer based communication systems, using a common information protocol. **Market migration to an all electronic, Smartphone based, financial transactions concept will have significant impact on conventional banking facilities. It will impact the physical attributes of the bank branch.**

Branch bank tellers for face-to-face transaction processing will disappear as they are replaced by remote smart devices, communications based, self service, transactions. It will significantly change the roll of branch banking personnel. It will reduce physical efforts such as mail delivery and processing. It will replace physical money and check needs with network/electronic based secure functions and strategies. Visits to the "branch" for transactions will be accomplished electronically. The business of Smartphone based banking will be 24/7. Successful bankers will need to move rapidly to keep up with the rapidly changing, remote, electronic functional environmental marketplace.

Forces for Change

The forces for migration of the bank to a Smartphone based role change will include: (1) the rapid growth of cell phones and Smartphones as the prime vehicle of individual communications, and their replacing transaction cards; (2) the role of the Internet as the dominant world wide communications network in almost all industries including bank, health, retail, education and government; (3) the disappearance of paper in the bank industry, including the growth of electronic money, check images, and remote/interactive self service; and (4) the migration of bank based Smartphone systems from stand alone facilities to Cloud systems with the removal of all geographic and physical boundaries. A Cloud system is the user's portion of a larger, internet based, remote computer system

Mobile Banking with Smartphones

Mobile banking is the use of a portable communications device to access and use financial services. This concept is well established with the use of wireless phones to find bank account balances and their status. As portable communications devices evolved into Smartphones, portable computers that allow phone calls, their banking functions are further increasing in sophistication. For example, Smartphones are now being used to capture and transmit check images for electronic deposits. The portable device also runs banking applications. For example, they can be used to calculate currency conversions and mortgage loan tables. Self service is the direct benefit of forty years of magnetic striped card based self service banking.

The Internet

The Internet, a world-wide communications network, allows access from more points, more quickly and more easily than any other network in the history of networks. Thus, along with its new facilities comes new and serious security exposures. The three most challenging are (1) preventing the misuse of lost or stolen smart devices; (2) preventing the effective use of overheard transmissions; and (3) preventing the downloading of fraudulent applications, Malware or viruses. Since there is no central authority dealing with these security exposures, the users must insure that they are protecting Internet plans and banking activity programs. Their actions must protect your Internet plans and programs. Please take this note of caution very seriously. There are security tools to protect your Internet actions. Your goal must be to use them effectively. They are the SPARC Security Solutions.

Executive Summary

Purpose: Provide a summary of this Book.

This report is intended to help you understand the use of Smart Devices, e.g. Smartphones, on the Internet in preparing for "Securing Your Internet Use". It is intended to introduce you to the Internet and its role, in the Internet based transactions and "Internet of Things" era.

The Internet

The Internet allows access from more points, more quickly and more easily than any other network in the history of networks. Thus, along with its new facilities comes new and serious security exposures. Since there is no central authority dealing with these security exposures, the users must insure that they are protecting Internet plans and banking activity programs. Their actions must protect your Internet plans and programs. There are security tools to protect your Internet actions. Your goal must be to use them effectively.

Card and Check Migration

Physical check entry to the bank disappeared with the advent of check image capture in ATM's, cell phones and Smartphones. However, the real test is the process by which the individual originates a "check-like" based payment. The payment needs to identify the payer and the payee. Where bills are being paid, the payee is identified by the demand for payment. The optical image feature of the Smartphone can be used to capture that data just as it is used to capture check images for processing.

The Plastic Card Equivalent Transaction

Use of the mobile banking device as a magnetic striped card equivalent signal source requires a wireless transmission from the mobile banking device to the signal accepting unit. A NFC, (Near Field Communications) signal is emitted by the mobile banking device. The mobile banking device displays multiple striped card equivalent type designations. A record is captured in the mobile banking unit for later reference, if needed. The acceptance device processes the "card-like" transaction into the banking system. The variable amount of the transaction is added to the signal transmitted in the NFC signal to the accepting device. The complete transaction data is then processed by the banking system.

Smartphone and Cloud Computing

Smartphone based Cloud computing is the delivery of common Smartphone based bank transaction business computer applications from a remote facility, online, through the Internet. These Smartphone based applications are accessed with a Web Browser. It uses software and data stored on servers (computer subsystems). The bank Cloud user rents a portion of the Cloud infrastructure from a third party. These Smartphone based Cloud processes reduce cost to the bank by sharing the Cloud computer power and resources. The bank does not have to provide added capacities for peak loads. The user must be concerned about the security of Cloud stored information and its protection.

Bank Organization of 2020

The primary, government-licensed, bank functional units (teller, loan and payments) will be the same in 2020. The primary changes of 2020 will be in the implementation of each transaction. The former implementation with paper based, manual processing and local handling will be replaced. They will be replaced by Smartphone based "electronic paper", transaction processing and remote Internet based processing. This will be achieved by the use of mobile transaction devices, use of the world wide Internet, and electronic logic implementation smart devices.

Internet Bank Accounts and Transactions

The all electronic bank of year 2020 will use the Internet to provide bank account records, access and all "branch" type functions and transactions for customers using the Internet. Smartphone based access to the 2020 bank, with all electronic accounts, will start with the URL (Internet address) of the Web page assigned to each customer's account. An explicit URL will be a unique Web page address for each customer's bank account. The customer's Web page, in turn, will provide direct access to all bank relations for that customer.

What is a Smartphone?

The simple, hand held, portable telephone has evolved into a hand held computer, Internet based, and providing phone functions. It is the result of decades of electronic component functional growth and physical size reduction. The simple, hand-held, portable telephone has evolved to a compact, fist-sized, computer capable of 95% of the function of your desk top computer. Its portability reaches any place you can contact cellular phone electromagnetic signals. Its computational ability exercises any programmable computer application within the capability of its operational program system. In other words, the room full of computers in past decades now operate efficiently in your palm as a Smartphone. Furthermore, it has a full display, a keyboard, an operating system and communications interface.

Credit Card on a Phone

The Smartphone uses NFC (Near Field Communications) capability to communicate with a transaction acceptor. The Smartphone is brought within 4 inches (or 10 centimeters) of the acceptor. Select card equivalent information. Initiate the emission of a selected transaction card. This is equivalent to swiping a magnetic striped transaction card through a card slot reader. To enable this transaction, the Smartphone contained application is opened with keying in a PIN, a personal identification number. The application allows loading the equivalent of multiple account information (card equivalents), within one Smartphone. This multiple account facility is used now in Southeast Asia countries and is spreading around the world. The NFC function allows two way communications. However, payment transactions are one way with account number going to the acceptor. Visa has tested this function in the United States and Southeast Asia.

Smartphone Applications

An application is a software program designed to produce a specific result or solution to an identified need. It may also be a computer configuration (input, computation and/or result use) designed to achieve a specific result. An application solution may also be the use of Smartphone functions and features designed to achieve a specific result.

Select and Execute an Application Program

Access the Smartphone's application directory for descriptions, prices, capacity requirements for storage and execution, display logo, network attachment, and performance needs. The selected applications are downloaded to the Smartphone. An identifying logo is displayed for later selection and execution. There are more than 400,000 Smartphone applications depending on the Smartphone and operating system you are using. To illustrate the range of applications, there is a list of the "must-own" Smartphone applications.

Familiarization (Based on the BlackBerry Smartphone).

Find the "On" button. It is generally in the lower right corner with a sun-like icon. It may also be a button in the upper left corner. When the button is depressed the screen becomes illuminated. The keyboard also becomes illuminated. Identify the speaker, microphone and earphone connection socket. On the reverse side find the removable cover for the battery and SIM card. The SIM card contains the information giving you access to a carrier and to a specific phone number. Moving the SIM card to another Smartphone gives it access to the identified phone number and carrier. Welcome to the world of thumb typing. Your thumbs enter information while the other fingers support the Smartphone.

Smartphone Politics.

The fast and successful pace of Smartphone usage growth attracts a number of interested parties, especially those associated with previous technologies and market entries.

All of the instruments associated with earlier solutions of the payment and marketing solutions will be impacted. Financial transaction cards, Smart Cards, ATMs, conventional retail marketing solutions, telephones, paper money, face to face Financial branch transactions and the conventional cash Register will all be impacted by the mobile Smartphone.

Aggressive, former industry groups will carve out a roll for them selves in this transition. For example, if their prior solution used integrated circuit chips, they will use that as evidence that they should automatically have a key role in the subsequent developments. That may not be entirely wrong. The Smartphone era will need standards.

The Unbanked and the Underbanked

Unbanked refers to any household or individual that does not make use of a financial institution for any type of financial or banking service or transaction. Underbanked are small businesses with access to financial services but do not use them. The Unbanked are reported as 10% of USA population. Underbanked are reported at an additional 15% of he USA population. These are currently reported as 28 million plus 45 million people. Both groups, the Unbanked and Underbanked, spend $130 million per year on alternative but relatively expensive financial services. These include check cashing services, pay day loans and money transfer services. Both have been seen as future business opportunities by most bankers.

New Smartphone Banking Role and Revenues

A remarkable characteristic of the Internet is the amount of free material available to anyone. Some providers, like Google, have evolved a plan to get advertisers to pay for the free results provided to its users. That is very much like the payment by advertisers for free radio broadcast programs which clearly identify the sponsor. However, it is expected that some web providers in the future will expect payment for their content. Bank services are paid for by the bank's customers in the form of loan and mortgage payments and the use of deposits.

Micropayments

Future bank services may need transaction payment amounts which are smaller in value. Similarly, Internet providers will need to avail themselves of techniques for collecting a larger volume of smaller amounts in payments.

Smartphone Economics 2020

The bank of 2020 will be considerably different with staff use and facilities. That will not necessarily reduce the cost of providing the bank. There will be major changes in the mechanization and supporting personnel. The physical branches size will decrease significantly. However, there will be expenses associated with smaller service facilities and remote Cloud facilities. There will be more expenses associated with maintaining the software and data bases need to support the new branch equivalent virtualization structure. Moving to the all electronic bank will also move the bank to a 24 hour, seven days per week response organization. The bank structure will be much more unattended. However, that requires operating facilities, power on, with fully operable communications and network services. Money will go into facilities to support this type of operation, their operating and maintenance staffs.

Security Architecture

As an Internet user, you must understand your own requirements. As a user, you must provide key information such as credit card numbers. The merchant provides important information in the form of receipts and payment information. Vital data flows in both directions. Hence, your security objectives must describe your possible exposures and your planned responses. A security

approach must be selected, implemented and the response evaluated for adequacy. Any solution will involve trade offs. The user must decide where to draw the line between expense and security adequacy.

PCI Security Standards Council

The Payment Card Industry Security Standards Council was founded by five global payment organizations. They are American Express, Discover Financial Services, JCB (Japan Card) International, MasterCard Worldwide, and Visa Inc.

The PCI DSS has six major objectives. A formal information security policy must be defined, maintained, and followed at all times and by all participants

Who is Who in Smartphone Based Mobile Banking

This is a list of software suppliers at the time this report was prepared. It is important to repeat a search of the Internet for the most recent list when you are preparing to use this information. This is a fast moving industry. Only the most current of search results will provide you with a current list of software suppliers.

Keyless Internet Processes

Forty years experience with magnetic striped cards, used with self service units ranging from mass transit to Automatic Tellers, demonstrates why 80% of the world's population is implementing self-service transactions in all industries. By contrast, 72% of our population are shopping on the Internet, but only 15% shop with multiple vendors. The need is for a "Keyless Internet Transaction" structure which can be understood and repeated with ONE use. That was the prime success factor for magnetic striped card use. The "keyless" process is demonstrated.

Traveling with a Smartphone

Historically, traveling meant leaving your entertainment devices at home – your music, your books, your reference materials, your movies and your TV. Today, they all travel with you, thanks to the Smartphone and networks. In addition, your Smartphone provides important assistance on your travels.

Smartphone User interface

The Smartphone display is the principle interface to the user. Its goal is to quickly communicate to the user the nature of the application and to enable quick user response for option selection, information entry and action initiation. As stated previously, the goal of effective user interaction is to achieve a "Learning Curve of One". The Smartphone display is probably the single most important element needed to achieve the "Learning Curve of One". This guide will try to provide suggestions to make more effective use of the display. They will highlight those display characteristics needed to aid in achieving that goal.

PCI-DSS Payment Card Industry – Data Security Standards

The Payment Card Industry (VISA, MasterCard, American Express, Discover and JCB (Japan Card Banks)) lists 12 requisites to maintain the security of payment card based transactions. The 12 requirements are in 6 areas, all of which are provided by the SPARC Security Solutions.

The Price of Not Using the SPARC Security Solutions

The price is two-fold. One is the requirement to investigate and understand the various attacks on the starting information content. There is the need to maintain the starting information content in a useable form. The second need is to continually educate card holding customers to their potential attacks. The card holders need to maintain continued vigilance against attacks and that takes education and technical support. Securing the Internet Use removes an important subset of attacks. Hence, reducing demands for card holder education and continued protection.

Changes and Banks

The bank's five year plan will continue to be a critical element of a successful bank strategy. However, experience dictates that any plan is valid only until its next annual review. Changes are introduced by the innovative bank leaders. New concepts emerge. Technology, information systems, delivery alternatives and applications move on to their next phase. Transaction scenarios adjust to market demands.

The secret of preparing for the future is to take today's best estimate and adjust annually to any reasonable and desirable change. The same applies to your plan. Results should be compared with the projected plan, and marketplace movement compared with your planning assumptions. In both the plan and it's building blocks, the important need is to adjust activities to market realities.

The customer interface will continue to be the crucial link in transaction success. That interface in 2020 will be as different as it was in prior decades. Think back and compare the differences. The changes are accelerating and the role of the banker is to stay ahead of the change process. To be forewarned is to be forearmed. The task is to recognize change for what it is - the demand for defining "customer convenience" and "business goals" content in a new time frame with improving technology.

Chapter 1

Fifty Years of Transaction Security Solutions

Purpose: Review Transaction Security Solutions Evolution
Action: Use the history to shape future efforts.

The Start:

The media based transaction device started in the late 19th century with the use of paper business cards for identification and transaction billing. Authorization of transactions in this formative period were via personal phone calls to a clerk in the card carrier's organization. The era of large volume machine readable transaction cards started later with the magnetic striped card development in 1966 and their first large scale market use in 1970. The first 250,000 magnetic striped cards were used in an airline ticketing test at O'Hare airport, Chicago, Il., in the first quarter of 1970. The cards were used in a pioneering self-service reservation and ticketing machine, from the IBM Advanced System Development Division, Los Gatos, CA at American Airlines with American Express magnetic striped plastic credit cards. Unfortunately, those striped cards cost more than $ 2.25 each to produce.

The Technology Selection:

The card developers quickly recognized a development dilemma. The card developers had to produce a single card solution that would work with both alphabetically accessed airline records and numerically based bank record access. Magnetic stripes were the only technology that had a multiple track capacity and a recording density capable of accommodating those multiple industry requirements. At the same time, the magnetic stripe was easily read and re-recordable. Security solutions such as encryption were quickly rejected due to their complexity and large execution time, the added Smart device expense and time required for a key based encryption process. The magnetic striped card plus a signature provided a two factor, dual control, security solution. Tokenization and de-identification techniques came later. Tokenization required a second device for transaction origination. De-identification used a process to hide the true identification of a message in transmission.

Data Based Control:

Use of a centrally maintained data base with consolidated activity recording became the preferred security solution for magnetic striped cards. More than thirty years of positive data base control experience has confirmed that original projection. During that period a new machine readable media technology was introduced every decade. The plastic card without stripes was used in the 1970s. The stripe was still too expensive. By the 1980s the striped card cost had fallen to an acceptable level, e.g. $ 0.25 each, with high volume production that allowed its mass distribution and use. The early 1980s also witnessed the introduction of large authorization networks by Visa, MasterCard and other card issuers. Their networks were designed to allow on-line point-of-sale units to connect directly to the data bases maintained by card issuer. The data bases collected all transaction values and locations. Simultaneously, in the early 1980's the Smart Card, with an imbedded micro circuit chip, was being developed in Japan and Germany.

Enter the Smart Card:

By the mid 1980s the North American based card associations networks faced a decision. Stay with their magnetic striped cards and their recently installed on-line networks, or migrate to the Smart Cards. Studies showed that a switch to Smart Cards, with their built-in PIN validation process would reduce installed network use by at least 75% since the Smart Card provided local PIN validation. In North America the card networks optioned to stay with magnetic stripes and their on-line networks. Outside North America the card issuers concluded that their less than perfect network performance dictated switching to Smart

Cards with their local Smart Card based, PIN based, authorization for most transactions.

The Cell Phones Arrived:

The next decade, (the 1990's), saw the introduction of the cell phone with its voice based authorization and the start of the Internet. The first decade of the smart phone followed with the development of Internet based shopping. The 2000's witnessed important changes in industry direction. With Smart phones, the consumer provided the infrastructure, the application programs and the Near Field Communications or Wi-Fi communications technology between the customer's device and the merchant's POS unit, which could be another smart phone.

The North American Magnetic Striped Cards Continued:

Much to the amazement of the original magnetic striped card developer, striped card use continued in United States into the 2010's decade. It lasted that long for two reasons. It provided a high volume use for the elaborate and expensive authorization networks. The other reason was that the data base controlled authorization system continued to provide adequate overall transaction security. Yes, there were successful attacks and losses, but a few percentage loss of total dollar sales volume was considered small and an acceptable cost of doing business. See an annual VISA report for specifics.

The New Challenges:

Along with the smart phone and the Internet came a new set of challenges. These included lost or stolen Smart Device units, over-heard transmissions and downloading on the Internet of fraudulent applications, malware and viruses. Unfortunately, the protection to date have been piecemeal solutions, e.g. encryption, after the fact device location or content erasure, and anti virus software. A recently patented security solution, the SPARC Security Solution ©, has introduced a new comprehensive transaction methodology security solution that does not use conventional PINs, passwords or encryption. However, it protects against all three Internet based security challenges.

The SPARC Security Solution:

The patented SPARC Security Solution combines three security techniques used successfully for more than 20 years. These are Dual Control, De-identification and Data Based Control. The three solution combination solves all three security challenges – Lost or Stolen smart device units, Over-heard transmissions and Downloading of fraudulent applications, malware and viruses – all without the use of conventional PINs, passwords or encryption. More information about the SPARC Security solution follows in this book.

Fifty years of progress has produced great progress in transaction security, speed and economics. However, sufficient challenges remain to seek further evolution of the responses to market needs for the next 50 years of transaction methodology evolution.

Chapter 2

The SPARC Security Solution (SSS) and Process Description

Purpose: Provide a complete SSS process description
Action: Use to examine all SPARC SS options:

The SPARC Security Solution combines three proven security solution (using a financial transaction sample):

Note: Steps added by the SPARC Security Solution are preceded by an #. Steps in the application program are denoted by a %.

!. Dual control:

Open the financial transfer transaction.
Enter the required fields:

Transfer to account number.
Enter amount.
#Enter the SPARC PIN of six characters.

%#The application generates the SPARC Security Number (the SIN):

%#The application unique identification number.
%#The Transaction number, a stored in the app.
%#The SPARC PIN is added to the true account no.(TAN)

2. De-Identification:

> %#The SIN replace the TAN in the transaction message.
> The transaction is transmitted via the Internet.
> The transaction arrives at Application Control Institute (ACI).

3. Data Base Control:

> %#The SIN is extracted and accesses the TAN data base.
> %#The TN of the SIN transaction number is validated.
> %#The SPARC PIN number is extracted and validated.
> The TAN is used to access the account data base.
> The transaction is processed.
> The up dated data base record is stored.
> The return confirmation transaction message is prepared.
> %#The return transaction number (TN) is prepared.
> %#The return SIN is prepared and inserted in the message.

4. De-Identification

> The return Transaction message is transmitted.
> The transaction arrives at the originating smart device.

5. Data Based Control.

> %#The SIN is extracted.
> %#The Application validates the return SIN.
> %#The transaction numberTN is extracted and validated.
> The transaction is completed.

Potential attacks:

> Lost or stolen unit lacks SPARC PIN.
> Overheard transmissions have incorrect SIN TN.
> Downloading fraudulent apps, malware or viruses lack proper SIN.

SPARC Security Solutions attributes:

100% compatible with existing standards and data bases.
Allows use of previous programs, data bases and devices.
Useable with any smart device and its operating system.
Does not use passwords, conventional PINs or encryption.
Lack of encryption allows use of lower cost smart devices.
#Minor application changes to provide and validate SINs.
Easy to understand with compatible standards format.
Doesn't require purchase of piecemeal security packages.
Allows use of lower cost Internet network.
Significantly reduces education needs for security functions.
Allows advertising security by SPARC Security Solutions.

Note: There are a number of data base systems available on the Internet for initial system installation.

Chapter 3

SPARC Security Solution – As Seen
By the SD User

Purpose: Demonstrate the SPARC SS simplicity
Action: Follow the SPARC Security Solution Transaction Process

Introduction:

Use a conventional Smart Device with an Android Operating system. Select a transaction application for a designated industry. For example, a financial transaction to transfer funds from your account to another account with the same bank.

Input to the Selected Transaction:

The application requests three entries. These are (1) The pay to account number, (2) The Dollar amount to be transferred. (3) Your six character SPARC PIN Code.

You transmit the transaction,

Almost immediately you receive the confirmation message from the bank. This includes a copy of the line entry. The same line entry appears in your monthly transaction report.

Chapter 4

SPARC SS Revenue Potential (SPARCrev)

Purpose: To Identify the SPARC Security Revenue Potential
Action: Establish and Realize the SPARCrev

The Opportunity:

There are a wide variety of revenue sources from SSS application. Here are examples:

Offer New Services:

>Secure vital data in files, DBs and transmissions.
>Offer secure Internet use services.
>Prevent Internet fraudulent downloading.
>Secure "Internet of Things" installations.
>Protect misuse of lost or stolen smart devices.
>Establish secure internet electronic post office.
>SPARCoogle for security info, advertising income.

Eliminate Costly Piecemeal Solutions:

>Eliminate encryption, antimalware, firewalls.
>Eliminate kill switches and recovery packages.

Improved Smart Devices Design:

>Cheaper units, smaller memories, slower speeds.
>Add internet interface isolation buffers.

The SPARCrev attack prevention opportunity (an example):

> This service protects an individual's Internet service from (1) effective use of a lost or stolen smart device; (2) use of overheard transmissions; and (3) downloading of fraudulent applications, malware and viruses.

The attack prevention service suggested costs $ 1 per month per email address and $ 0.02 per Internet transaction. The economics of this new and important service follows:

Wikipedia; Internet Available Statistics (from authoritative industry sources footnoted in Wikipedia):

The world's population:	7.22 Billion
Internet Users:	3.04 Billion
USA Internet Users:	0.28 Billion
Internet transactions per user:	12,500/year (1,042/month)
Assume 10% USA penetration:	28 Million users
Revenue at $12 / user/yr:	$ 336 million annual charge
($ 1/month/user)	
Revenue at $ 0.02/transaction:	$ 7.0 Billion
Total USA Revenue:	$ 7.3 Billion per year
Outside the US world wide Internet users:	
Assume 1% penetration:	28 Million Users
Total Non USA Revenue:	$ 7.0 Billion per year

That is $ 14.3 Billion per year with only 10% penetration of USA Internet users and 1% outside the USA willing to pay a small amount to obtain secure attack prevention Internet usage. That is (1) no effective use of lost or stolen Smart Devices. (2) no effective use of over-heard transmissions; and (3) prevents down loading of fraudulent applications, malware and viruses.

SPARCrev Revenue Attributes and Implementation.

More important, this revenue is produced without branch offices, without a sizable marketing organization and without the need for a sizable implementing organization.

This arrangement is easily set up. Use the client's usual email address for the service. When received, the email message is scanned with an anti-malware detecting program. The volume of transaction activity is recorded for automatic billing/payment. The clean email is then forwarded with a SPARC Identification Number to a second email address set up to receive clean email from this service. That arrangement can be established on a totally automatic and remote basis.

The other SPARCrev attributes include:

No conventional PINs, passwords or encryption are required. That allows use of less expensive smart device units, compatible with current transaction standards. Dropping encryption allows use of a slower and reduce memory smart device. This creates a "Secure Internet Operation" while using existing system communications & Data Base products.

SPARCrev appears to be the only comprehensive security solution available.

No smart device or operating system modification is needed.

The SPARC Security Solution is easily added to existing systems. The SSS works with all smart devices & their operating systems. The SSS is based on security techniques with greater than 20 years installed experience. This solution (and patents) work with all industry transaction systems, "SPARCInternet of things" and unsolicited transactions.

SSS provides BEFORE the fact Lost or Stolen device protection. Most industry solutions work "AFTER the fact". It is easily understood and implemented. Patented with alternative implementations. Secures Internet use, Also "Internet of Things", This avoids the need for piece meal solutions, e.g. encryption. However, SSS also avoids encryption key management issues.

The Information by-product: The anti-malware scanning process provides a wealth of useful information. Types, sources, and traits.

Chapter 5

Dealing with Hybrid Environments

Purpose: Describe the approach to Securing Hybrid Environments
Action: Apply for a Patent to secure Hybrid environments with SSS

What is the Hybrid Environment?

We live in a very complex society. Amazon Books lists 250,000 books on the Internet. 25,000 of those books pertain to Internet Security. There are many proposed solutions. Some are very narrow with single problem solutions such as Encryption. Others discuss "Before the Fact" solutions. Those prevent a problem before they occur. Other discuss "After the Fact" solutions such as "Kill Switches" or stolen device tracking. Some solutions are installed. Others are to be installed. Some security solutions are focused on one industry's needs, such as banking or retail. Others focus on functional system security needs such as "transaction" or "Internet of Things" systems. There are other alternatives based on providers or historic achievements. One further factor forces a Hybrid environment. It takes time for a complete security solution to be installed in a geographically dispersed or multiple location organization.

Dealing with Hybrid environments

This environment is dealt with in one of two ways. One is to keep an inventory of known security solution participants. Those are the "easy" participants with whom to deal. The second approach, for the rest of the potential population is to use an inquiry based communication.

The SPARC Security Solution interfaces to a variety of usage situations. These include:

Transaction systems dealing with application control institute (ACI), e.g. a bank with a data based control system. This solution generates and uses a SPARC Identification Number (a SIN). The SIN consists of the security application's or device's unique number

"Internet of things" Systems. Dealing with Internet connected source or recipient with each source or recipient interfaced to the Internet through a SPARC SS chip or a logic device. That chip/logic device relies on an inventory of know recipients and a synchronized time test of the transaction receipt.

Smart device to smart device transfers. These are secured with the same concept as used with "Internet of Things". Namely, each an inventory of know recipients and a time synchronized reception test. In this process, unsecured smart devices fail the security test and their messages are isolated until they join the security process. They may be communicated with an unsecured process, but by then their exposure is known, "before the fact".

In addition to the various types of security environments, here are several added security issues. Namely, solution details and algorithms are used to generate SIN and TN. Allowing a thief to order these applications should NOT provide access to the SPARC Security Solution implementing knowhow. Although there is the need to protect vital data in the messages. That includes government and other key numbers or data. These protections are achieved by these steps:

1. The TN generation occurs only in the protected area of the ACI data base system. When generated on demand, it includes a "time of issue", as with the IOT security process. That result goes to the unsecured recipient and is then returned to the ACI, where it is time interval checked.

2. Vital data is protected by adding the true account number (TAN) of 40 digits to the Vital Data using absolute arithmetic (no arithmetic carries). The TAN is not carried in the message. Hence, an over-herd transmission is fully protected.

Patent action required:

The necessary patent action was taken with the "Internet of Things" patent action. At most, the patent action needs one more sentence. Namely, add a sentence that states the "Internet of things" patent application also applies to dealing with uninsured smart devices in a smart device to smart device interaction SPARC Security Solution.

Chapter 6

Why You Need this Book

Purpose: Prepare readers to understand why they need SSS
Action: Have a good understanding of your required actions.

The Old Solutions Providers:

A large number of firms are still selling the old piecemeal solutions. That includes the Encryptors, the Firewalls, the malware detectors, kill switches and the like. They want to continue selling their inadequate offerings. The smart devices providers want to sell you the larger memories and faster calculators needed for the old solutions. Another group that wants you to continue using dedicated networks. They want the Internet security challenges not to be attractive to your use despite their lower costs and world wide access.

The Hybrid Environment Challenges

Most companies offer a set of mobile applications. Let me suggest a simple test for those company executives who might be interested in why they should act. What are the current activity statistics with these company provided applications?

1) How many of their customers' smart devices were reported lost or stolen in the past year? What have been the resulting losses – by the customers – or by the company?
2) How many attempts have been made to reuse overheard transmissions from smart devices? With what resulting losses?

3) How many of their customers reported usage problems of downloaded fraudulent applications, malware or viruses? With what reported losses?

4) Who pays how much for the smart devices to install piecemeal security packages such as encryption, firewalls, virus detection and repair, post loss remote finding or remote usage killing?

5) Who pays how much to upgrade customers' smart devices to implement encryption? (More memory and faster internal speed).

These questions will tell the company executives how serious is their need to understand this security subject. These are all good reasons to use the SPARC Security Solutions.

Note: Smart Devices include all sorts of smart phones, tablets, phablets, and any other stored program operated devices.

Chapter 7

This is a Smart Device

Purpose: To describe the Smart Device and examine its use.
Action: To provide a Smart Device selection basis.

Smart Device Evolution

The simple, hand held, portable telephone has evolved into a hand held computer, Internet based, and providing phone functions. It is the result of decades of electronic component functional growth and physical size reduction. The simple, hand-held, portable telephone has evolved to a compact, fist-sized, computer capable of 95% of the function of your desk top computer. Its portability reaches any place you can contact a network offering mobile phone electromagnetic signals. Its computational ability exercises any programmable computer application within the capability of its operational program system. In other words, the room full of computers in past decades now operate efficiently in your palm as a Smart Device. Furthermore, it has a full display, a keyboard, and communications interface.

Smart Device Acceptance

Recent executive surveys indicate that more than 80% of Smart Device using executives would reach for their Smart Device before their morning cup of coffee. Most executives (over 80%), would conduct business on their Mobile Phone before their desk phone. Family wise, their 8 years old children have already asked for their own Mobile Phone. You are likely to provide it to your 8 year old child for safety purposes, to allow their frequent family socializing and to provide instant access to their roaming. Some Smart Devices incorporate geographic positional sensing (GPS) to enable parents to quickly locate, physically, their children, to further enhance their Mobile Phone based safety. The built-in geographic position sensing has been used to very successfully track and locate lost or stolen Smart Devices.

Major Smart Device Component Parts

The Smart Device is a complete communications based computer system with a variety of input and output components. It is used to execute a variety of application programs intended to provide the user with specific set of transaction related plans and results. Some of the applications are used for general financial results such as currency conversion, measurement conversions, and travel options. Other applications may be used for personal subjects of interest to the Smart Device owner. The major Smart Device components include:

A compact physical container/structure.
    Protects components from weather and moisture.

Power supply – converts battery output to component power needs.

Power storage, e.g. a battery.

Display: Electronic and color with touch sensitive screen. A variety of on-screen symbols for applications and function identification and selection.

Communications interface and antenna
Digital, programmable computer
Wireless/contactless interface
Keyboards, function buttons and switches.
Microphone and speaker; Headset jack.
SIM card tray (defines communication/carrier protocol).
Manufacturer's labels

Other possible components:
    Solar mobiles for power
    Physical access key
    Cover to protect antenna operation
    Cord loop for carrying
    Plastic card reading slot (stripe or contacts)
    Finger grips
    Battery access and cover.
    Display light level control
    Speaker/Headset volume control
    Headset jack
    Display scroll control

It is important to read the instructions provided by the manufacturer to identify all components and controls. Using the Smart Device, identify all components and controls. You should be able to identify and use them without looking at the unit. That degree of familiarity will assure your complete understanding of the unit you acquire and plan to use.

What is a Mobile Phone?

There are three types of hand held communications devices.

The Personal Digital Assistant (PDA) has wireless capabilities. It uses Wi-Fi or Bluetooth. Wi-Fi is the trademark of the Wi-Fi Alliance of manufacturers providing wireless local area networks based on an IEEE 802.11 standard. Bluetooth is an open wireless technology for short distances created by Ericsson and managed by the Bluetooth Special Interest Group. The second type of hand held communications device is the Mobile Phone (CP) which has PDA (Personal Digital Assistant) capabilities but communicates with mobile communications facilities. The third type is the Smart Device (SP) which is an Internet based, programmable computer, that has all the Mobile Phone (CP) communications capabilities.

There are two types of mobile networks. GSM (Global System for Mobile communications) is used by 80% of the global mobile market. It is used by more than 4.3 billion people across more than 212 countries.

This digital technique is considered second generation (2G). CDMA (Code Division Multiple Access) uses a spread spectrum technique that allows multiple messages on the same channel. Phones intended to work on one network type do not generally work on the other.

Some network providers require you to purchase a matching phone from them. Ask before purchasing. It is possible to "Unlock" a phone. That allows the phone to work with any network. It is possible to buy an unlocking service to enable your phone to work with other networks. Most mobile providers subsidize the phone purchase price as a means to lock you into a multi-year contract. Hence, buying a phone from another source, a manufacturer or private party, may be more expensive. However, it allows you a more flexible arrangement in choosing or changing carriers. In fact, it allows you to buy prepaid amounts of communications, which is generally the least expensive arrangement.

Styles of Smart Devices.

Mobile phones are available in a variety of physical shapes and layouts. They generally differ in display and keyboard/data entry features. For each style, you can find GSM and CDMA network using units. The trick is to identify your desired carrier first, and then find a mobile phone to match your interface needs and operating requirements.

These Smart Devices May Use A Stylus (Touchscreen)

Traditional Style:

This type of phone style generally has a large screen which provides text entry using an on-screen, software based, keypad. This operation is generally supported by the use of Windows Mobile software. It's disadvantage is that it may be a bit awkward to use as a mobile phone. You may wish to use a headset for better phone communication. Try it!

Thumb-pad Style

This style offers a square screen on top of an almost equal size thumb-pad type keyboard. It does not offer an on-screen key board even though it has a touch screen for interaction. It works well as a mobile phone and generally does not require headset use. Its smaller screen shows less information. Its thumb-pad keyboard may be difficult to use or to dial numbers for operators with large hands. Try it!

Slider Style:

The screen strongly resembles the "Traditional" PDA. The screens are generally smaller which makes the better for use as a phone. The keyboard is retracted and hidden when used as a phone. The full QWERTY keyboard is revealed by sliding it out. When slid out the image on the screen changes automatically from "portrait" to "landscape". Most mobile providers have a version of this phone. It is similar to the "Traditional" PDA. It's software is usually compatible. The keyboard is larger than the "Thumb pad". The "Slide" works well as a phone. There is a large selection of useful Windows Mobile software. The slider can be boxy. Not all application programs support both portrait and landscape display modes.

iPad Style

This is a large surface touch screen. The screen is occupied with the logo for each application program acquired. The screen also may be scrolled with finger movement to get to applications beyond the initial screen capacity. The unit is a handy mobile phone size. Care must be taken not to damage the screen. The screen also needs to be cleaned from many finger marks accumulated in its use. The user needs to memorize the meaning of the content for each logo. Since there are more than 400,000 application candidates, that memorization can be challenging.

The Following Smart Devices Do Not Use A Stylus

Thumb Pad Style

Microsoft calls these units Smart Devices. All software actions are done by hardware buttons. This phone has been popular because these units are very compact and slim. Operation is geared to a one handed usage. The display is not a touch screen. Software must be written for a non touch device and those programs are more limited. The thumb-pad works well as a phone. However, the lack of a touch screen may be considered awkward by some users. People with large fingers may have trouble dialing numbers and the software may be limited. Try it!

Flip Phone Style:

This is a "Clamshell" type phone. Text entry is time consuming as it uses a "T9" text entry. This method of text entry requires multiple key strokes for each character. This unit does not have a touch screen. Hence, software is more limited. Touch screen software will not work on this style mobile phone. The unit has an excellent shape for use as a phone. However, the text entry without a touch screen can be very time consuming. A small screen and limited software may make this unit difficult to use.

Candy Bar Style

This is a less common mobile phone style. It uses the time consuming "T9" multiple key entry per character. It lacks a touch screen and software is generally limited. However, it has an excellent shape for phone use. Lack of a touch screen and limited software make this unit difficult to use.

Picking a Mobile Phone

Consider these three factors, in this order:

1): The Carrier: do they provide the geographic coverage, communications features and the economic alternatives you require?
2): The Mobile Phone or Smart Device features and functions: Does the unit have display, interactive functions and the features you need?
3): The Software: Do the functions and features match your phone characteristics (e.g. touch screen vs key entry). Does the software also offer the growth of functions and applications you

may need later, such as navigating, messaging, multi-media, and service support.

The Global Smartphone shipments are projected to be 2 billion units in 2018. In 2013, 76% of Smartphone shipments used the Android Operating System.

Smartphone Nomenclature

There are a set of terms and abbreviations used to describe Smartphones, as follows:

Apple "G": The product generation.
Others "G": The product's network speed.
App: Abbreviation for application, a pre programmed solution to provide a specific end result.
CDMA: Wireless standard for Verizon and Sprint.
GSM: Wireless standard for AT&T and T Mobile.
Wi-Fi: Local connection signal
OS: Operating System. Android for Google. iOS for Apple.
BBM: Blackberry messenger for pictures, videos and voice notes.
iPad Mini: Apple's small tablet with 7.9" display.

Buying a mobile phone.

Smart Devices are becoming more complex and more like mini computers. What counts is what goes on inside of them. Consider the basic features:

1) The Processor: Phone performance is dependent on processor speed. The faster, the better. High end Smart Devices generally come equipped with a 1 GHZ processor.
2) The RAM: The more Random Access Memory capacity, the better able the Smart Device to do multi-tasking. High-end phones have at least 512 MB of RAM.
3) The Display Screen: There are two important types of touch screens – Resistive and Capacitive. The Capacitive is considered

faster and responds to human touch. The Resistive screen can be used with devices like a stylus.

The OLED and AMOLED screens give strong color with amazing brightness when used indoors but fade when used indoors. Super AMOLED has fixed that problem. AMOLED is also good for watching TV. TFTLCD screens have an inadequate viewing angle, present faded blacks, and low brightness levels. A screen size of 3.2 to 3.5 inches is the best viewing size and is easily carried in pockets and purses.

4) Check the keyboard: These are a personal, preference, whether real or virtual. Do you touch type or hunt and peck? Do you need tactile feedback from a key depression?
5) The platform and application software: Which applications best suit your needs? Check the software options and usage before making a final decision.

The Smart Device Usage Challenges

There are two sets of challenges with Smart Devices. One set relates to your selection and use of a pocket computer interfacing a variety of communication alternatives. Included are:

Smart Device selection and usage training
Smart Device economics.
Smart Devices rules and policies – employer and employee.
Care and feeding of a sophisticated electronic device e.g SIM card and battery change
Control and maintenance of the Smart Device.
Transition to later models.

The other set of challenges relate to managing a number of Smart Devices interconnected to a business organization, including:

Application development and evolution
"Unlocking" units to accept other networks applications
"Jail Breaking" to switch communications networks.
Communications support and evolution

Maintenance and service
Cost of operation and usage
    Employee units and customer units
Device and network management
Employee training and monitoring
Managing upgrading and evolution
Privacy and security requirements

Smart Device Operation

Your interface to the Smart Device are your eyes and fingers. Your eyes identify icons on the screen, locate action buttons or screen touch points. Your eyes read messages, symbols and labels. With the large number of Smart Devices available, there are several alternatives actions possible to achieve a given operation on a Smart Device. For example, in one case a rotating knob will be a volume control. In another Smart Device, a touch sensitive moving marker on the screen may produce the same volume control result. These two devices give equivalent operation. You must discover the mechanism used in the Smart Device you are handling.

Chapter 8

The Internet Role In Transactions

Purpose: An introduction to the Internet.
Action: Establish your transaction's focus on the Internet.

An Internet Note of Caution:

Internet components – applications, services, devices, technologies, vendors, users, protocols and standards – grow and change each year. This description focuses on the elements critical for your successful secure use of the Internet. However, this material needs to be updated when used. Key Web page addresses, (Domain names or Uniform Resource Locators), URLs are included to help you quickly assess the latest transaction status. A key industry information source is the Internet Retailer Guide to E-Commerce Technology (internetretailer.com). There are similar guides in other transaction based industries.

What is the Internet?

The Internet allows transaction access from more points, more quickly and more easily than any other network in the history of networks. Thus, along with its new facilities comes new and serious security exposures. Since there is no central authority dealing with these security exposures, you, the user, must insure that you are protecting your Internet plans and programs. This chapter will describe your Internet facilities. The chapter on security will describe the options for your action to protect your Internet plans and programs.

Please take this note of caution very seriously. There are many so-called security tools to protect your Internet actions. Your goal must be to select the effective tools and then to use them effectively.

The Internet Initially:

The Internet was an electronically connected set of computers with a common information structure, format and information encoding. It was intended to share available computer time between government supported computer installations. The objective was to use their surplus available computer time to solve large computational problems associates with atomic energy development. It was also intended to provide an ability to share facilities in case part of the facilities were destroyed. The communications structure was enlarged to include access to their libraries and development records maintained in each of the participating organizations.

Eventually – Today

The Internet is interconnected public networks that are self supporting and run on a cooperative basis. All share a common data format and content code. That is a protocol called TCP/IP (transmission control protocol/Internet protocol). The international association of companies that manage the Internet is called the World Wide Web (www).

Web Pages and Other Nomenclature:

The Internet provides Web pages. A Web page is a collection of text, graphics, sound and, sometimes, video. Together, they create a single window of scrollable materials. Hypertext is the text used on a Web page that leads the user to other related information, or Web pages. The Web page is found by a Browser. That is the software used to find and access a Web page.

URL or Domain Name: The Web page address on the Internet is called URL, a Uniform Resource Locator. The URL is the designation used by the Browser to access a Web page. Where does the URL come from? It may be found in the output of a Search function. It might be provided by the Web page provider to guide others directly to a Web page of direct interest such as a bank, retailer or health services provider. It may be found in publications, press reports, or directories. As with any "address" it will be found with most communications vehicles.

Domain is another designation for the address of a Web site. It may be more than an address. If well selected, it may also be descriptive of the organization it addresses. The Domain name consists of several parts. The letters www. at the beginning of the domain name indicates the following information is an address on the World Wide Web. The last two or three letters of the Domain name indicate the category of the organization named. It may be com. commercial, or gov. government, or org. organization, or one of several others. The latter designation may be followed by a designation of the country location of the originator, such as .us for United States, .au for Australia and .jp for Japan.

Email:

The most widely used internet application is email. That is a message with a stated Internet destination and from an Internet source. It is also a vital marketing tool.

It drives business results in the form of increased traffic, customer awareness and customer involvement. A recent Internet Retailer study showed more than 40% of business leaders were planning to increase their email marketing budgets. It will expand with a double digit expansion rate for the next five years. Why? Email is inexpensive. Email is effective because customers rely on it and marketing gets better results from its use. It is a frequent carrier of related URL's. The Internet lacks any security for the user's device, the URL, or the email transaction message content.

Favorite Function

An important function of the Browser is the "Favorite Function" (FF). It is a record of specific Web pages for recall later to provide quick Browser reentry to a Web page previously designated with the Favorite Function. It is a quick recall of a specific Web page, without going through a Web page search and discovery process. That discovery process would require a search operation and a search sequence output stream examination. Use of the Favorite Function enables applications in all industries to go directly to a Web page of interest.

Use of the Favorite Function for a Transaction Application:

An Internet based industry provides each customer with a URL which uniquely identifies the location of the customer's industry data on the Internet. Using the URL in a Browser takes the user to an entry point for that industry's transaction activities. The entry Web page will immediately impose further security control on access to the designated Web page. The software may ask for a Personal Identification number (PIN), a password established earlier, or a more exotic biometric device output such as a fingerprint reader.

Successfully providing the entry control information, the program now allows a spectrum of industry's functions. These range from simple inquiries to sophisticated requests and control reviews. There may be subsequent control features that respond to larger transaction values, value transfer request actions and sound industry transaction criteria.

Specialized Networks

There are hundreds of specialized uses of the Internet. These are a subset of Internet use designed to interact with selected groups of individuals, corporations, religious, country residents, government agencies and the like. Their function is to allow the specialized participants to meet, exchange information and socially interact. Popular "Social Networks" include Twitter, Facebook, MySpace and LinkEdit. These networks offer low cost communications (plus the cost of the needed access equipment and software). In some instances, these networks reach up to two-thirds of a group's participants. Care must be taken to avoid or protect sensitive information. Participants need to establish and maintain lists of participants they want to reach in each type of network. From a marketing point-of-view these are excellent vehicles for marketing for new clients.

The Internet is Essential for Transaction Solutions:

The Internet is the vital element that ties all of the Smartphone transaction units together into a working system. It allows the Smartphone unit to reach all of the data elements and software elements that combine to provide the transaction services to the Smartphone user. Smartphone transactions provides significant productivity improvements to the transaction based industry. Your knowledge of the Internet and its role in Smartphone transaction based systems are essential for you to successfully build these working systems, and to realize their important results.

Chapter 9

Keyless Retail Transactions

Purpose: To describe work reducing functions available.
Action: Use work reducing steps in Internet transactions.

The Retail transaction:

Forty years experience with magnetic striped cards, used with self service units ranging from mass transit to Automatic Tellers, demonstrates why 80% of the world's population is implementing self-service transactions in all industries. By contrast, 72% of our population are shopping on the Internet, but only 15% shop with multiple vendors. The need is for a "Keyless Internet Transaction" structure which can be understood and repeated with ONE use. That was the prime success factor for magnetic striped card use.

Transactions on the Internet remain complex. A retail purchase requires up to 25 steps. Half of the steps require data entry keying and three steps require users to examine the results of long search responses. The use of improved solutions such as Amazon's "1 click" reduce these efforts by one half, which is still 12 steps and 2 searches.

Conventional Internet Transaction

Placing a conventional retail transaction through the Internet is a 15 to 20 keyed steps process. The process would include these steps:

> Search for a search engine.
> Select a search engine.

Search for a vendor.
Select a vendor.
Search for a desired item to be purchased.
Select the item to be purchased.
Select the item's style.
Select the item's size.
Select the item's color.
Select the quantity.
Select the delivery method.
Select delivery option.
Enter delivery address and postal zone.
Confirm acceptance of the total charge.
Select payment alternative.
Select credit card to be used.
Enter payment amount information.
Approve payment process and amount.
Print invoice and shipment information.

The Smartphone Introduces New Function

The Smartphone based, keyless process starts with information stored in the Smartphone. Included are: (1) The user's preferred payment information; (2) The user's preferred shipping requirements; and (3) the user's preferred email address for communications.

"Frequent Favorite" is a form of browser based function which provides direct Internet access, generally listed in a sequence of URL's. When one is selected, it provides an appropriate Internet web page address (URL). The URL automatically directs the user's Internet browser unit to the web page describing the article, service or subject being considered for acquisition. Use of this feature bypasses the need for using search engines and scanning long streams of search results. Without any keying, the browsers presents the web page showing the URL identified item. Beyond that, the order options, e.g. color, size and so forth, are selected by using a mouse. The order completion information for payment and shipping are provided by Smartphone stored content.

Keyless Shopping Speeds Purchasing Internet Acquisitions

This Smartphone supported function is a time savor. By bypassing the need for searches and examining search outputs is a browser function provided by most browsers.

Your use of this Smartphone supported function will substantially speed your internet access and getting results on a more timely basis.

Chapter 10

SPARCpay

Purpose: Smart Devices with NFC offer many payment options
Action: Use your Smart Device for payments.

Your Smart Device (SD) with Near Field Communications (NFC) offers a number of payment options in conjunction with your financial service institute, also known as your Application Control Institute (ACI). The simplest example is a funds transfer to another account. That application requests the payee account number and the amount of funds to be transferred. The sequence of steps that followed that application entry were described in detail in chapter 2, "The SPARC Security Solutions".

There are a number of similar applications for:

Payment at a point of sale.
Payment at a retail check out.
Payment at a supermarket check out.
Payment or withdrawal at an ATM.
Payment at a transit gate.
Payment in a taxi cab.
Payment by bumping with another Smart Device.
Receipt of funds by bumping from another Smart Device.

The Internet Payment Challenges:

The SPARCpay process is protected by the SPARC Security Solutions. Those protections require you to use a dual control to open the SPARCpay application. Depending on your choice, that requires entry of a SPARC Pin, or the use of a second security application or the use of a security device. Any of those prevent the effective use of your Smart Device if it is lost or stolen. SPARCpay also prevents the effective use of an over heard transmission. It also prevents the downloading into your Smart Device of a fraudulent application, malware or viruses.

Other SPARCpay options

Your ACI will provide you with a number of other pay options including check deposits, loan and mortgage payments and automatic bill payments. All are protected by the SPARC Security Solutions.

Chapter 11

Securing an "Internet of Things" (IOT)

Purpose: Explain IOT operation, security challenges and the SPARC
   Security Solutions responses.
Action: Communicate the steps necessary to secure an IOT.

What is an Internet of Things?

Gartner forecasts the IOT will be 26 billion units talking to each
other via the Internet by 2020. These are a wide range of devices
exchanging information via the internet. The Internet provides lower
cost communications. Unfortunately, it also provides a series of security
challenges. These include:

   Down loading of fraudulent applications. Malware & viruses.
   The fraudulent applications may be designed to:

      Usurp control.
      Steal industrial knowhow.
      Sabotage or misdirect device operation.
      Provide misleading responses.

What is the SPARC Security Solution for an Internet based IOT?

The SSS inserts a logic device between each unit and the Internet. The
logic device maybe a custom chip, a dedicated logic unit or a smart
device application. In an IOT situation there will be a "Sender" and a
"Receiver". Both units are bidirectional.

What are the SSS messages?

The SSS IOT sender message consists of:

The 40 digit SPARC Identification Number (the SIN).

The Sender's unique identification.
The message send time on a 24 hour basis.
The message send date.
The message transaction number (non sequential).

The security challenges are to prevent a counterfeit message or a replay of an overheard message transmission from fooling the receiving unit.

The IOT receiving unit provides these tests before accepting the incoming message: These are:

From an acceptable source? This requires the receiver to maintain a list of acceptable sources.

Within an acceptable time period from the sending time? This requires the receive to have an internal clock, and a time synchronizing mechanism. Also, this requires an acceptable maximum interval for each physical location. An acceptable interval will be set for moving receivers.

With the correct transaction number? This requires storage of the last sequence number, a sequencing algorithm and a next sequence number calculator.

Note that the acceptable time interval may be a fraction of a second from transmission to receipt. That requires that the acceptable interval must be set for each IOT based on its physical dimensions. The acceptable time interval is never transmitted. However, the participating units may require a periodic resynchronization of all clocks in a given IOT such as daily.

How is vital data protected?

Vital data is protected by a protection value kept with the expected sources list. The vital data is added to the protection value at the sender. The protection value is NOT transmitted. Upon receipt at the receiver, the protection value is subtracted from the protected value to recover the vital data.

Complete Logic Diagram:

Detailed Design, Sender and Receiver logic units from US Patent Application number US 2015/0249663 A1, dated September 3, 2015, Figure 14.

Summary of SPARC Security Solution IOT Attributes:

This process does not require the use of PINs, passwords or encryption. The Sender Identification Number is the controlling mechanism. This allows use of lower cost and simplified logic devices.

This process is 100% compatible with transaction processing and data base standards.

Copied or counterfeit messages will be rejected by the logic tests.

Downloaded fraudulent applications, malware and viruses are rejected for lack of an acceptable SPARC Identification Number.

Useable with all "Things", communications technologies, and logic technologies. Improves the market for IOT devices.

Increases the usability and output revenues of the Internet which decreases IOT costs and operating expenses.

Chapter 12

SPARC Health

Purpose: Personal health record.(PHR).
Purpose: Identify the PHR Content

The Content

The content of a personal health record are described in two national standards. They are the Standard Guide for Content and Structure of the Electronic Health Record – ASTM E1384, and Coded Values for the Electronic Health Record – ASTM 1633.

The Internet record – NCBI.NLM.NIH.GOV/PMC/Articles/ PHC2047330/.

Provides a detail record of the prescribed content.

What is the content of the PHR?

This is a collection of information about your health. This is not the same as the electronic medical records which are owned by doctor's offices, hospitals, and health insurance plans. Your PHR includes anything to help you manage your health. It generally includes:

Your medical identifications.
Your primary care doctors' names and phone numbers.
Allergies, including drug allergies.
Your medications including dosages.
Chronic health problems. Your problem list.
Major surgeries with dates.

Living will or advanced directives.
Family history.
Immunization history.
Consultations
Physician's orders
Hospital stays: Operative and pathology reports. Discharge summaries
Imaging and X-ray reports
Lab reports
Consent and authorization reports

Also added may be information about disease prevention. This may include:

Results of screening tests.
Cholesterol and blood pressure.
Exercise and dietary habits.
Health goals, such as stopping smoking or losing weight.

The personal health record allows you to share information. It also helps you to manage your health between doctor visits. It enables you to:

Track and assess your health.
Make the most of your doctor visits.
Manage your health between visits.
Get and stay organized for your health activities.

The SPARC Security Solutions role:

This is a transaction/data base system (See chapter 11). Items of data are protected from source to data base. They are added to the data base with confirmation message to the source. They are accessible by inquiries from known sources.

Chapter 13

Implications of Introducing Internet security

Purpose: To Anticipate Market reaction to Improved Security
Action: Use changes to guide future investments/actions.

The Historic Evolution of Dedicated Networks:

Historically, the lack of Internet security has been solved in two ways. One way to switch to the use of dedicated networks. Two examples are the credit card networks for VISA and MasterCard. In both cases the dedicated networks were used to capture transactions and to authorize transactions. Furthermore, "Securing Your Internet Use" also has implications in the future design of Smart Devices.

Dedicated networks incorporate network electronics to assure and maintain network security. However, this requires continued monitoring to assure no change in the security status. It also requires continued alertness to equipment erosion or failure. These are world wide networks. That means there is continued surveillance in a wide range of geographic conditions. These are not inexpensive endeavors.

The Historic Development of Piecemeal Solutions:

A large number of programs were developed to solve specific Internet network security challenges. Included are commercially available programs to encrypt and de-encrypt message content, anti-malware detection and suppression programs, and viruses detection, firewalls and virus suppression programs.

In addition to their cost, these specialized programs require annual renewal and, more importantly, they require periodic updating to reflect their continued change of attacks and their required correction techniques.

After a Secure Internet Introduction

Detection and correction of an Internet based security attack is not the end of the problem. Transaction messages carry vital data such as social security numbers, tax identification numbers and even re-ordering information. All of these vital numbers will need to be protected even in a "secure" Internet environment. Yes, even a secure Internet environment still requires the use of assorted technique for protecting vital information. There will also be the development of new attack techniques. Further improvements in De-Identification, in achieving dual control and improvement in data based controlled applications will be needed to improve their speed and application.

Impact on Future Smart Devices Design:

An important lesson from the subject patents and this text is the need to isolate incoming transactions and transaction results until their security is validated. Those incoming transactions need to be isolated until the questioned transactions satisfy the SPARC Identification Number (the SIN) tests. The isolation buffers in future Smart Devices will hold and isolate the questionable materials. That will play a valuable role in SPARC Security Solution implementation. This will also provide an opportunity to notify the transaction source of the disposition of the transaction they sent.

Life is a Good Example

Through the ages professions such as medicine have continued to evolve. Identification of new challenges, development of new responses will be required and education of new professionals will be a continued need. Welcome to the real world! The battle may shift but even the change to a more secure environment will have its new challenges.

Chapter 14

Good reasons To De-Identify

Purpose: Explain the reasons to use De-identify
Action: Use for all SPARC Security Solution applications.

The Source:

The following reasons for using De-Identification as part of the SPARC Security Solution are from an IBM report "6 Good reasons to De-Identify Data".

What is De-Identify?

This is the data left after the directly identifying data has been removed. The remaining data can no longer be associated with a specific account number (TAN). That also means none of the remaining data can be used to research the missing identification. That requires that secondary identification data, such as a social security numbers, also must be removed or disguised. The disguise may be easily accomplished by adding the true account number (the TAN) to the secondary identification data using "absolute" arithmetic. The TAN is not transmitted. It is available in the Application Control Institute's data base when needed for re identification.

Why Use De-Identify?

The six good reasons to use De-Identification are:

1. Allows the remaining data to be used in many ways.

2. Allows the remaining data to be used for marketing research.
3. Allows the remaining materials to be used for medical research without violating privacy.
4. Protects privacy of the material sources even if the materials disposition is not authorized.
5. Significantly reduces the risk of legal compliance infractions.
6. Demonstrates due diligence even if a privacy breach is alleged.

Why our Interest?

As with seat belts in cars, other safeguards should be used including safe driving and proper maintenance of the vehicle.
That means rational care of the smart device. Also, taking reasonable steps to prevent its loss or it being stolen.

This material is taken from an "IBM for Midsize Business" program intended to provide midsize businesses with tools, expertise and solutions they need.

Chapter 15

SPARC Bit Stream Processing

Purpose: Understanding the distribution of entertainment content.
Action: Provide SPARC SS benefits for Bit Streaming.

What is Bit Streaming?

Bit Streaming is the distribution of a continuous flow of Information such as motion picture content, performance events and live sports events. Bit streaming distribution is an important source of revenue producing entertainment content. Bit streaming is usually distributed through the Internet. With that transmission comes all the usual Internet challenges. Those include malware, viruses, overheard transmissions and unapproved bit streaming access and copying.

How does SPARC Security Solutions secure Bit Streaming?

The SPARC Security Solution protects the bit streaming with two numbers. One is the SPARC Identification Number (the SIN). This is a standard's compatible value of 40 digits. Included in the SIN is the unique identification number of the SPARC Security service provider. The second number is the transaction number portion of the SIN. This is a unique number which is changed for each application of Bit Streaming protection process.

How is the SPARC Security Solution applied?

The account number is NOT transmitted in the clear. Rather the bit stream is identified by the applicable SIN. In addition, the bit stream is disguised by adding the true account number, which is not transmitted, in 40 digit increments to the bit stream. At the receiving location the true account number is subtracted from the secured bit stream in 40 digit increments. In other words, the bit stream was protected by a simple De-Identification process.

There is a more direct solution. It requires using a logic device between the Internet and the display device that implements the SPARC Security Solution process. That is the same logic device design that is used to protect individual devices linked to the "Internet of Things".

Chapter 16

SPARCloud Security Solution

Purpose: To describe the Application of SSS to Secure Clouds
Action: Apply SPARCloud SS to Large Cloud Installations

What is Cloud Computing?

Cloud computing is the provision of computing power as a service, rather than as a specific computer product. A simple analogy is electric power. Electric power come from a plug in the wall rather than building, maintaining and delivering power from our own power plant.

How is it Accessed?

Cloud computing requires the delivery of vast amounts of data through the Internet or through dedicated networks. In either case the delivery process is subject to the usual assortment of security attacks. These may involve stealing vital data, attacks with fraudulent applications, malware or viruses. Also overhearing wireless transmissions and attempting to fraudulently reuse the captured vital data.

Applying the SPARC Security Solution:

Cloud based data is moved in fixed size blocks. Each block has a SPARC Identity Number (a SIN). The SIN is 100% compatible with the Transaction standards. There is a cloud maintained data base of known and acceptable SINs. Each incoming cloud data block adds its assigned SIN to the data base. Part of the SIN includes a redundancy check for the entire data block. The SIN is validated each time the data block is accessed or moved. Blocks leaving the cloud are also SIN checked.

Failure to validate the SPARC SS SIN results in a defective block destruction or retransmission of the data block. Any redundancy check failure indicates an addition or removal of data to the original data block. If needed, redundant cloud block retransmission may be used or a more complete content validation or recovery content.

Summary:

SPARCloud is built on the same SPARC Security Solution principals. Dual Controls are based on controlling data bases and specific SIN based block numbers. The SIN based block numbers complete the De-Identification process. Thus, the SPARC Security Process completes its secure handling of the SPARCloud computing data flow security process.

Chapter 17

Securing Unsolicited Messages

Purpose: To anticipate an Internet fact-of-life Action:
Action: Prepare an Unsolicited messages plan of action.

The Internet Challenge:

Dealing with the Internet occasionally results in a flow of unsolicited messages. They may be quickly identified by the absence of an acceptable SPARC Identification Number (SIN). The presence of an acceptable SIN indicates prior handling of the message with SPARC Security Solution rules, de-identification and data based controls.

Unsolicited messages may be fraudulent transactions, malware or viruses. As such, they represent a significant danger to the receiving applications or systems.

Unsolicited Messages Plan Of Action:

Processing of unsolicited messages is 100% compatible with the processing of all messages. Unsolicited messages should be segregated and stored separately. They should immediately scanned by a free program such as the "Malwarebytes" anti-malware program. A contaminated message should be destroyed immediately with a record of the message disposition sent to the sender. An uncontaminated message can be provided with a correct SIN and processed in a normal SSS manner.

Chapter 18

Introducing SPARCoogle – a Free Security Service

Purpose: Use SPARC Security Solutions to Attract Advertising $
Action: Establish the SPARCoogle Organization

What is SPARCoogle?

SPARCoogle is the availability of SPARC Security Solution knowhow for no charge to the requestors. This will be a direct result of the growth of SPARC SS experience and the vast communications of SPARC SS usage benefits. What type of information will be available uniquely through SPARCoogle?

> Educational materials provided by SPARC SS insurance companies.
> SPARC SS registration options and Internet addresses.
> Sources of SPARC SS additional materials such as multi-language instruction manuals, planning materials, and reporting materials.

Is There A SPARCoogle Advertising organization?

> One of the great contributions of the Google organization was the demonstration that advertiser will support this type of service with a large amount of paid advertising.
> SPARCoogle organization includes:

> Advertising receipt and processing.
> SPARCoogle Internet Network design.
> A SPARCoogle Internet browser.
> Setup and maintenance of SPARCoogle data base.
> Setup and maintenance of a multi-language data base.

Setup and maintenance of a world-wide operation.
Negotiate a cross license and access with GOOGLE.
Setup, maintain $ for future SPARC contributions.
Setup, maintain press interface for SPARCoogle.
SPARCoogle education materials, process.
Setup an annual contribution recognition event, awards.

Chapter 19

SPARC Security Solutions Questions and Answers

Purpose: Provide frequently asked questions with answers.
Action: Use to prepare responses to frequent questions.

Introduction:

Payment processes and technologies change rapidly. Historically, they have changed every decade for the past 50 years. I was fortunate to have lead the effort to create the magnetic striped cards almost 50 years ago (1966 to 1973). The stripe content and the supporting data based authorization architecture we architected then have now evolved with several generations of card technologies. All indications are they will continue to provide the usage decision base for this vital industry. The following material demonstrates their ability to support the coming era of smart devices. Magnetic striped cards are 50 years old. Smart cards with PINs and chips are now approaching 35 years of age. Now is the time to recognize the rapid shift to smart devices. The following material is offered to demonstrate that the rapid change should be encouraged and welcome. With it comes the ability to secure the use of the Internet, a very welcomed event. I wish all the users of these proposals the same sense of contribution to society that I feel. Jerome Svigals.

SPARC Security Solutions (SSS) ®, a Questions and Answers Compendium ©2015.

Q. What is the SPARC Security Solution (SSS)?

A. SSS provides an enhanced method to assure for secure wireless and Internet based transactions. SSS uses a combination of three security processes which have been used by industry for more than 20 years, with a SSS provided innovative and patented improvement. The entire transaction world is moving rapidly to the use of smart (programmable) devices, such as smart phones or tablets. The SPARC Security Solution allows use of a lower cost smart device. SPARC does NOT require the use of PINs, passwords or encryption. SPARC protects against the three most serious smart device security challenges: (1) Lost or stolen units (50% in the USA last year); (2) Misuse of overheard transmissions; and (3) Down loading of fraudulent applications, malware and viruses. SSS does NOT require smart device or operating system modification. It is 100% compatible with existing industry transaction standards and data bases.

Q. Why would using the SSS be valuable in my business?

A. Use of smart devices is becoming a factor of life for anyone over eight years old. Even those not served by a bank and the under banked are smart device users for transactions with employment and family. Smart Devices are an infrastructure provided by the users, rather than by the application provider, e.g. a bank. Hence, all industries will benefit for an improved security solution for smart devices. Thus, SSS offers improved economics, a single solution for the three major smart devices security challenges, and is useable with the existing major investments in networks, data bases and products (hardware and software). More important, SSS departs from previous security solutions which were piecemeal, expensive, usually after-the-fact and destructive solutions.

Q. What is unique about SSS?

A. It's patented features. This is primarily the "SPARC Security ID" concept and use. The three security solutions used by SPARC have been used successfully for more than 20 years, world-wide. They are (1) Dual control; (2) De-Identification (initially a US Government medical specimens patent); and (3) Data based control. The SSS advances are its simplicity, economics, 100% compatibility with existing processes and data bases. SSS uses proven techniques with its unique ability to avoid use of old, piecemeal and expensive security solutions. SSS ability allows use of the low cost, universal Internet rather than expensive dedicated networks. This makes SSS <u>unique</u>. You will not need to use Virus Detection programs or Encryption programs. This SSS attribute is true for all smart devices, their operating systems and applications in ALL industries.

Q. Do we employ encryption?

A. No. We employ De-Identification. This is a <u>secure</u> process used by the federal government for more than 20 years in the healthcare industry to prevent source identification of medical samples. Encryption requires substantially more storage, higher performance and increased cost in a smart device. De-identification also includes techniques for protecting vital data.

Q. Do we employ tokenization?

A. No. Tokenization is replacing an identification or account number with a random number. SSS uses an uniquely and patented constructed version of the historic transaction processing standard account number to replace the true account number (TAN).

Q. Do we use multifactor authentication?

A. We use the long used basic dual control, the fundamental security technique of the financial industry, e.g. card and PIN.

Q. Who uses the SSS solution today?

A. Everyone. We use the basic security techniques now in use. SSS simply redefines the account number content, which is the SSS patented highlight. SSS uses a 40 year old, cross industry account number and data base contained standardized identification number.

Q. What proof do we have that it works?

A. The account number based data base systems have been successfully used for forty years, world-wide. For example, it is used by every card issuing institution to authorize transactions. The latest Nilson Report puts current credit card losses at $0.06 per $ 100 of gross sales. That is a remarkably small loss ratio, considering decades of fraud development techniques.

Q. When will SSS have proof?

A. SSS has proof now by use in existing systems. Proof will be further confirmed when we obtain Underwriter's Laboratories Transaction Security certification early next spring.

Q. How to validate the strength of solution?

A. SSS is confirmed by current industry usage. The SSS enhanced security functions will be further confirmed by UL Transaction Security certification.

Q. How to subscribe or build SSS myself?

A. You will build SSS your self as all industries now do. You will need to make a minor addition to your data base and a minor modification to smart device applications. This inserts the SSS process into smart device use. No modifications are required to the operating system.

Q. How is SSS configured in all industries?

A. SSS uses existing processes.

Q. What is the SSS time line?

A. SSS is In use now. SSS requires minor application modification to incorporate the patented definition of the SPARC Secure ID Number (SIN) and process.

Q. Will your use of SSS be unique in your industry?

A. No. You will be the first to take advantage of SSS secure functional improvements and economics? Eventually, others will follow your leadership.

Q. How often will SSS have new releases?

A. It is difficult to have new releases with security techniques which are 20 or more years in use. What will be new will be the added industry application uses and devices that you will now incorporate in these well established SPARC security solutions.

Q. What influences new SSS releases?

A. You will control how you apply the SSS.

Q. How to handle SSS maintenance and enhancements?

A. SSS is based on existing industry standards with established processes for handling maintenance and enhancements.

Q. Is SSS adequately capitalized?

A. Since the SSS is based on existing standards, all industries will bear the burden with a minimum of guidance. SSS will lead by application development, not by expensive product development. This allows low cost use of the SSS functionality. This greatly reduces the SSS capitalization requirements.

Q. How are you protected if SSS sells to your competitors?

A. That is like asking the electric company to not provide power to your competition. The fact of life is that this simple, low cost, universally applicable and effective SSS will eventually be used by all. Your challenge will be to keep ahead of industry progress and lead your competition into the new Secure Smart Devices applications within the SSS era.

Jerome Svigals

(Leader of the 1966-73 IBM magnetic striped card development team, stripe multi-track data content architecture and data based security architecture used world wide for more than 30 years. Member ABA and ANSI standards groups for magnetic striped card specs and content). Re US Patents 8,453,223, dated 5/28/13, 8,806,603, dated 8/12/14, 8,997,188, dated 3/31/15 and 9,009,807 dated 4/14/15.

Chapter 20

Use of Prior Security Solutions, Standards, Programs

Purpose: Reconfirm that SSS is 100% past solutions compatible
Action: None is required after reconfirmation of compatibility.

Introduction:

This will be the shortest chapter. Fully compatibility gives you the option of using all previously available products. For example, SPARC Security Solutions De-Identification provides adequate content security. However, if you wish to also use encryption, do it. It is a redundant effort, but do it if you feel more comfortable. After a while, you will recognize your redundant efforts. This includes Malware detection, Encryption, Firewalls, Viruses Detection and elimination, Fraudulent application detection and elimination, and so forth.

Chapter 21

Summary of SPARC Security Solution Patents

Purpose: Identify Basic SSS Patents & Their Application
Action: Use Application Definitions to Identify Market Use.

Summary of SPARC Patents Claims:

8,453,223 dated 052813: System to verify transaction content with a one-time identifier. Provides Dual Control on transaction origination. Independent of Smart Device and Operating System. Generates SPARC Identification Number used for De-Identification. Uses Data Base Control to recover True Account Number from SPARC Identification Number.

8,806,603 dated 081214: System to verify a transaction which is biometrically actuated. Wireless. One-time identifier. separate to and from the application control institution. Using NFC. For a plurality of devices (This is IOT). Works with magnetic striped media.

8,997,188 dated 033115: Protects unsolicited transactions. Protects without use of PINs, passwords or encryption. Destroys invalid transactions. Transaction count NOT incremented by one. (Prevents use of over-heard transmission). Accepts transactions based on time. (An IOT security feature).

9,009,807 dated 041415: Works with external devices. Determines if source of transaction is acceptable (This is also IOT). Modifies the smart device to include a buffer to temporarily store a message until validated. Includes an alarm when smart device and dual control security device are too far apart physically.

These are the major claims. There are a number of claims of less significance.

Patent Pending:

2015/0249663 published 090315: Patent Application for "Security for the Internet of Things". Listing 23 claims. "An application control device controls another device."

Chapter 22

SPARC Security Solution Smart Device Simulation.

Purpose: Demonstrate The SPARC Security Solution
Action: Use the simulation to demonstrate SPARC SS.

SPARC Security Solution Simulation:

(Note: this is a patented process)

> Requires two Android Smart Phones, Smart Device 1, (SD1) and
> Smart Device 2 (SD2):
> One is the transaction device SD1 with two applications. The
> second, SD2 is the Application Control Institute, e.g. the bank,
> with two applications.
>
> > App 1: Application is a financial transaction.
> > App 2: Application is the SPARC Security App.

The Process:

SD 1, App 1: Creates the transaction with the TAN.
SD 1, App 2: Completes the transaction by generating SIN.
SD 1, App 1: Assembles, transmits the transaction with SIN.
Internet: Carries the Transaction to SD 2.
SD 2, App 3: Receives the transaction.
SD 2, App 2: Validates the transaction, with the SIN.
SD 2, App 3: Processes the transaction with the TAN.
SD 2, App 3: Creates return transaction with SIN2.
SD 2, App 2: Completes the transaction

SD 2, App 3: Assembles and transmits the transaction.
Internet: Carries the transaction to SD 1.
SD 1, App 1: Receives the transaction, replaces SIN2 with the TAN.
SD 1, App 2: Validates the transaction.
SD 1, App 2: Completes the transaction.

The App Details:

(SD 1)	(SD 1/2)	(SD 2)
Smart Device	SPARC SS app	Application Cntrl Inst.

Open fin trans App 1:
Enter app info
(pay to, amount,
SPARC PIN)
Send request to App 2 SSS

        Open SSS App 2
        Enter SPARC PIN 6 Char.
        Generate SIN (SPARC Identification Number)
        Gen TN+!, Store (transaction number)
        Send SIN to SD1

Replace TAN with SIN (True account number)
Send Trnsactn to ACI (Application control institute, e.g.bank)

                Open trnsactn\
                Extract SIN
                Seek SIN Record
                Extract True Acct No
                Extract TN
                Validate Trans TN
                Access TN
                Process TN transaction
                Gen return msg
                Send return Msg

Rec Msg
Extract SIN

Send to SIN to SSD app
                  Receive SIN
                  Extract TN
                  Validate TN
                  Calculate T+1
                  Send Msg to SD
Rec msg, Complete Trans.

Chapter 23

SPARC Security Solutions versus Foreign Hackers

Purpose: Describe past Internet attacks and SPARC SS response
Action: Use SPARC SS knowledge to prevent a reoccurrence.

The Report

The New York Times reported (8/12/14) that foreign hackers had successfully amassed 1.2 billion Web credentials (user names and passwords) from an Internet based attack. The attack amassed 4.5 billion records.

Let's Assume

That they caught an equivalent amount of SPARC Security Solution based transaction. What would they have?

They would have messages without true account numbers.
No PINs, passwords or encryption processes or results.
The transaction numbers are out of sequence.
There are no readable user names or vital data.
Data base responses or overheard transmissions are not usable.
No Smart Devices access information.
In summary, they would have captured nothing of value.

Chapter 24

SPARC Security Process Key Numbers (SIN and TN)

Purpose: Describe key components of SPARC Security Solutions
Action: Test SSS by full disclosure.

Where did it all start?

The basic security concept originated fifty years ago with the development of the magnetic stripe. The challenge with striped cards was to interface to a minimum of two different control systems. One was the numeric based banking systems with account numbers. The second was the name based travel industry systems with alphabetic name access. These became the basis for many future standards. The first was ISO 2984 in 1983. It had three tracks, but the numeric Track Two became the finance industry basic. It consisted of 40 numeric digits of 5 bits each. The primary account number is 19 digits. There is an added 12 digits for miscellaneous number fields. The remainder of the track digits are used for control sentinels.

Through The Intervening Years

As the transaction medium changed from cards to smart cards to smart devices, the subsequent standards' content remained the same to protect the resulting authorizing data bases. The design of the SPARC Security Solution choose to use the same format for its SPARC Identification Number, the SIN. Use of the SIN allowed full use of existing data bases, devices, software and systems. However, there was a remaining challenge. Fraudulent access to the SIN by over-hearing, or use of a lost or stolen smart device required a further solution.

The Need for a Further Identification Variable:

The added challenges of over-hearing misuse of data and use of lost or stolen Smart Devices were solved with the use of a transaction number of 4 digits in the SIN. For example use of a SIN value twice has an acceptable account number, except for the duplication of the TN. Hence, the four digit TN is an added precaution for several attack scenarios.

The added TN value requires an algorithm to advanced the sequence. The algorithm must. avoid making the algorithm known to a thief with his own Smart Device. That is avoided by advancing the TN value by algorithm only at the Application Control Institution (ACI) data base.

Protecting Vital Data:

The De-Identification process does not protect vital data in the "protected" record or transaction record. This may include telephone numbers, government services numbers such as social security, and a variety of passwords, financial identification numbers such as credit cards, and PINs and other security access codes. These may be protected by a very simple but secure process. The De-Identified message LACKS the true account number for the transaction record being protected. Hence, if the data to be protected is added to the true account number in 40 digits or 20 alphabetic characters segments. The process is called "absolute" arithmetic which does NOT do a decimal carry between digits. The process is easily reversed when it is necessary to recover the vital data at the ACI.

Future Key Numbers

The future will see further attacks on the key numbers. Corrective steps to future attacks will occur when needed.

Chapter 25

Securing against Ransom Ware and other Malware

Purpose: Prepare to recognize and reject malware.
Action: Eliminate recognized malware.

What is Ransom Ware and Malware?

Malware is a computer program that is designed to do unwanted or destructive actions not requested by the computer user or owner. The malware programs come through the Internet as a routine download. They have a number of other troublesome capabilities. They reproduce themselves. They make unauthorized copies and redistribute them on the Internet. In short, they have the ability to perform many undesirable activities as a routine part of Internet downloads.

The dangers and possibility of recovering from Ransom Ware

Ransom Ware is malware with the added ability to encrypted or hide vital data and then offer to recover it in return for a demanded ransom. Unfortunately, paying the ransom may not result in recovery of the hidden data. Ransom Ware comes in many forms but all have the same negative characteristics. These are just more types of viruses found on the Internet.

Malware Defenses:

The most effective response to malware is backing up your data frequently. That requires diligent backup schedules. An even more effective defense is to perform the backup on an external drive that can be disconnected from the Internet when not doing backup. Keeping your operating system up to date will also provide a recovery capability. A good operating system will also include a system restore function to assist in system recovery when attacked.

An important function is to exercise back up even if an attack is not detected. In that way you will build your confidence in your defensive tools.

Chapter 26

Underwriter's Laboratory Secure Transaction Listing

Purpose: Explain UL Role
Action: Obtain UL Transaction Security listing

Who is UL?

UL is an international organization. It sets operating and performance standards for articles used in homes, offices and factories. It offers testing of articles against the standards definition. The testing results are made widely available. Perhaps, their most important use is in the Insurance industry where the results are used to set insurance rates. (See Wikipedia for a more comprehensive discussion of the UL role).

Transaction Security:

A recent addition to the UL standards is one for Transaction Security. This testing function for chip related products and systems includes:

POS testing
ATM testing
Brand testing
Card personalization testing
Handset testing for networks attachment testing
Mobile secure element testing, and
ISO functional testing.

These tests assure interoperability, a major step preceding productive operation. These steps assure the test candidates that they will meet the requirements of a very competitive marketplace.

More details are available from services.ul.com on the Internet.

Chapter 27

Using Partial SYIU Solutions

Purpose: Describe use of a partial usage solution.
Action: Take advantage of SSS in more situations.

The Usual Situation:

The SPARC Security Solution is designed for use in a complete transaction. That includes initiation, transmission, processing, return transmission and completion. What is an incomplete transaction? For example: Initiating a transaction that does not require a completion.

The incomplete transaction, such as a posting of information, is still subject to the Internet challenges. It must still secure a transaction from a Lost or Stolen device. In must still prevent the effective use of an over heard transmission. It must still prevent the "up loading" of fraudulent applications, malware or viruses to the Application Control Institute.

The other processes that may be partial include IOT, multiple ACI's and payments. Each is handled as the partial transmission process. Since the protection is in the application program, the protection continues until the application is ended, completely or partially.

The objective is to make the application as complete as possible with the SPARC SS protection functions. That assures the maximum survival of the SSS protection functions.

Chapter 28

Complying with Payment Card Industry Data Security Standard

Purpose: Comply with PCI Data SS
Action: Demonstrate conformance.

The PCI DSS Requirement:

Control Objective:	PCI DSS Requirements:
Build and maintain a secure network	1. Install and maintain a firewall configuration to protect cardholder data.
	2. Do not use vendor supplied defaults for system passwords and other security parameters.
Protect cardholder data.	3. Protect stored card holder data.
	4. Encrypt transmission of cardholder data across open public networks.
Maintain a vulnerability management programs.	5. Use and regularly update anti-virus software on all systems commonly affected by malware.
	6. Develop and maintain secure Systems and applications.
Implement strong access control measures.	7. Restrict access to cardholder data by business need-to-know.
	8. Assign a unique ID to each person with computer access.

Regularly monitor and
test networks.

9. Restrict physical access to
    cardholder data.
10. Track and monitor all access to
    network resources and
    cardholder data.
11. Regularly test security systems
    and processes.

Maintain an information
security policy.

12. Maintain a policy that
    addresses information security.

Who are the PCI?

They are the major branded credit card schemes of VISA, MasterCard,
American Express, Discover and JCB (Japan Card Business).

How does SPARC Security Solutions conform to PCI DSS?

Let's start with a review of the SSS process:

The SSS transaction process starts with a DUAL CONTROL The Smart
Phone transaction process starts with (1) Two Smart Phone applications;
or (2) Two smart phones; or (3) A Smart Phone and a Security Device.
Those actions create a SPARC Identification Number (the SIN) which
replaces the True Account Number for DE-IDENTIFICATION.

The De-Identified message is transmitted via the Internet to the
Application Control Institute (ACI), e.g. the bank. The ACI uses DATA
BASED CONTROL to recover the true account number. The ACI
processes the transaction and reverses the process. A return SIN is
computed. The return message is de-identified. The return message
has its SIN validated Dual Control and the transaction is completed.

How has the 12 Step PCI DSS Process been completed?:

1. SIN validation before acting creates a firewall.
2. There is no use of a password.
3. ACI stored cardholder data access requires a SIN validation.

4. Encryption is replaced by a De-Identified message.
5. Acceptance is limited to SIN validated messages, hence resisting fraudulent applications, malware or viruses.
6. SPARC Security Solutions offers a secure system for application access.
7. Access to cardholder data requires SIN validation.
8. Each access device and user has a unique SIN.
9. Physical access to cardholder data requires a validated SIN.
10. All access required SIN validation and identification.
11. User processes allow regular system testing.
12. Installing and using SPARC SS is a clear security process.

Other PCI DSS based Payment Security Offerings

Accertify
ACI Universal
Authorize.net
Braintree
Cybersource
EBAY Enterprise
Paypal
Shopify
Symantec
Thawte
Trust Guard
Vantiv

Summary: The SPARC SS offering is unique. It is 100% compatible with existing transaction security standards and data based controls. It works with all Smart Devices and their operating systems without modification. It uses security processes with over 20 years demonstrated success.

Chapter 29

The Price of NOT Using The SPARC Security Solution

Purpose: Demonstrate Complexity NOT Required by SPARC
Action: Issues Avoided as a Specific Result of Adopting SPARC

Major Bank's Message to Smart Phone accepting merchants:

Beware of Data Compromise as a merchant.

What is Data Compromise?
Steps to take when suspicious of data compromise.

Contain and limit the exposure.
Provide notification to Bank's executive.
Follow legal requirements to government authorities.

What happens during a data compromise investigation.

Forensic investigation.
Report findings.
Identify accounts at risk.
Merchants determine fines and liabilities.
Comply with the PCI DSS – validate PCI compliance.

Is it a Common Point of Purchase (CPP)?

A source of multiple fraudulent transactions.
Where did the fraud take place?

Who reported the fraudulent activity?
What does a CPP do?
What does the bank do for a reported CPP?

Understand your PCI compliance requirements.

Major Bank's message to smart phone using customers:

Don't be fooled by an imposter
Stay away from a hard sell
Don't adopt a pet password
Put up a shield
Use common sense
Open with care
Be on the lookout
Use internal controls
Guard your bank's ID and password.
Protect your self on line
Log on frequently
Understand bank's security provisions.
Understand mobile products and services.

Chapter 30

All Again In Summary

Purpose: Describe a new Smart Device security solution.
Action: Add this application to your smart device.

The Internet Challenges:

Use of the Internet is very attractive. It offers a world-wide, low cost access to the world. However, with the use of Smart Devices it has three serious challenges. (1) The using Smart Devices are Lost or Stolen. That was 50% last year in the United States and higher elsewhere. (2) The wireless transmission from the Smart Device to the Internet interface unit, although only 10 centimeters distance with NFC, along with legitimate downloads, is over-heard and the transmissions are stolen for fraudulent reuse. (3) The Internet use is not secured and often provides downloads of fraudulent applications, malware and viruses, among the legitimate downloads.

Securing a Transaction System:

How do we secure credit card transactions? The secret is two-fold. Each credit card has a forty digit true account number (TAN). That is used to access a data base which contains all the reported transactions for the card. That combines two security techniques. One is a card plus a signature or SPARC SS 6 character PIN code. That is dual control. Second is the compilation of card activity in a data base. This security solution has been used by most card issuers for more than 30 years with losses contained to less than 1% of total sales. (See the latest VISA annual report).

The Magic 40 Digits:

The 40 digits contain, in card usage, an issuer identification, a unique card number identification and some discretionary data such as the card expiration date. The SPARC Security Solution in a smart device uses a separate security application with a unique security number for each user. This SPARC Security Number (the SIN) is used in the message to the data base in place of the TAN. This process is called De-Identification based on a US Government patent of twenty years ago. The Dual Control is achieved by requiring a 6 character SPARC PIN entry to the security application. It then provides the SIN to replace the TAN in the transaction message to the data base controller. The SIN carries the SPARC PIN entry for evaluation at the data base and a Transaction Number (TN).

When received at the data base controller, the SIN is used to recover the TAN, validate the SPARC PIN TN and the transaction is processed. The return process to the Smart Device reverses the process. In summary, the use of two applications and a SPARC PIN to initiate the transaction prevents the effective use of the smart device if it is lost or stolen. The use of the SIN in place of the TAN prevents an over-heard transmission from being effectively use. Use of the SIN at the data base or in the return message allows the system to separate a genuine transaction, with a valid SIN, from downloading of fraudulent applications, malware or viruses, all of which lack a valid SIN.

This a patented process. However, individual users are granted a free usage license. Anyone else should contact smartcard@sprynet.com for a low cost license. For a complete description of the process, including protection of important data such as social security numbers, contact us.

A SPARC Security Solutions Glossary

Purpose: Provide the definition of new terms
Action: Provide the terms used in a new application area.

SPARC Security Solutions Report Used Terms:

Apple Pay: An Apple Corporation provided smart device using NFC communications to initiate secure payments.

Attributes: A quality or features regarded as a characteristic of something.

Bit Stream: A sequence of binary digits sent over a communications path, such as a television show.

BYOD Secure: Securing your own provided device.

Cardware: A style of software distribution.

Cloud: A data center connected to the Internet.

Cyber attacks: An unauthorized security attack on a computer or communications network.

Data based control: Using cumulative account activity to assess account security status or transaction validity.

De-Identification: Removal of elements connecting data with its source. Patented by the US Government.

Dual Control: A security process requiring two processes or actions to gain authorization or to enable a process.

Easy pay: A digital payments device or program.

Fraudulent application: A smart device program designed to perpetrate an illegal purpose.

Hacker: One who uses software to gain access to or to cause damage to a computer system or via the Internet.

Identification Insurance: Financial protection against identification theft.

iDoctor: A set of digital tools for use by a physician. (Accessible using UTube).

I pal 6: An Apple Corporation provided Smart Device.

Malware: A smart device program designed to be harmful, usually delivered via the Internet.

Marketing manager: A customer definition or sales based action plan director.

Pay: To give value.

PIN: A personal identification number of 4 digits.

Power point: A software program to provide a multiple screen presentation.

Product manager: A device definition or family of devices plan director.

Security: Protection from distortion, abuse or any type of attack.

SIN: SPARC Identification Number. Confoms to the International standard for transaction account number (TAN).

SPARC PIN: A six alphabetical characters code for secure application access.

Things: Smart devices that interface to the Internet. Usually with two devices interacting.

Viruses: A smart device program capable of copying itself and corrupting a computer system or destroying data.

SPARC Report terms NOT used:

Authentication: A security process using two means of identification.

Encryption: A key driven data encoding process.

Multiple factor authentication: A security process using more than one means of identification.

Tokenization: Using a random number to replace a True Account Number.

CPSIA information can be obtained
at www.ICGtesting.com
Printed in the USA
BVHW080238110119
537596BV00001B/117/P

9 781514 449677